HOW DO ELECTRIC MOTORS WORK?

PHYSICS BOOKS FOR KIDS

CHILDREN'S PHYSICS BOOKS

Speedy Publishing LLC

40 E. Main St. #1156

Newark, DE 19711

www.speedypublishing.com

Copyright 2017

All Rights reserved. No part of this book may be reproduced or used in any way or form or by any means whether electronic or mechanical, this means that you cannot record or photocopy any material ideas or tips that are provided in this book.

In this book, we're going to talk about how electric motors work. So, let's get right to it!

WHY ARE ELECTRIC MOTORS IMPORTANT?

Electric motors are one of the greatest inventions in history. People during ancient times would have been fascinated by electric motors. Before electric motors, everything had to be done by hand or driven by animals.

Electric Motorcycle

If you look around the room you're in, you'll probably find lots of electric motors. For example, your computer has at least two. There's one to power your drive and another to operate a fan that cools the computer.

If you check out the kitchen, you might find a dishwasher, an electric can opener, a coffee grinder, and a microwave. All of these have electric motors. An electric shaver and a hair dryer both have motors run by electricity. Ceiling fans, air conditioners, garage openers, and washing machines all have electric motors. If you go all around your home, you may find as many as 20 to 50 electric motors. You might even have an electric car!

Kitchen appliances

Electric drill

Even the smallest electric motors feel heavy. The reason is they have a lot of copper and magnets on the inside of them. If you get some old appliances and pull them apart, you can get a better idea how

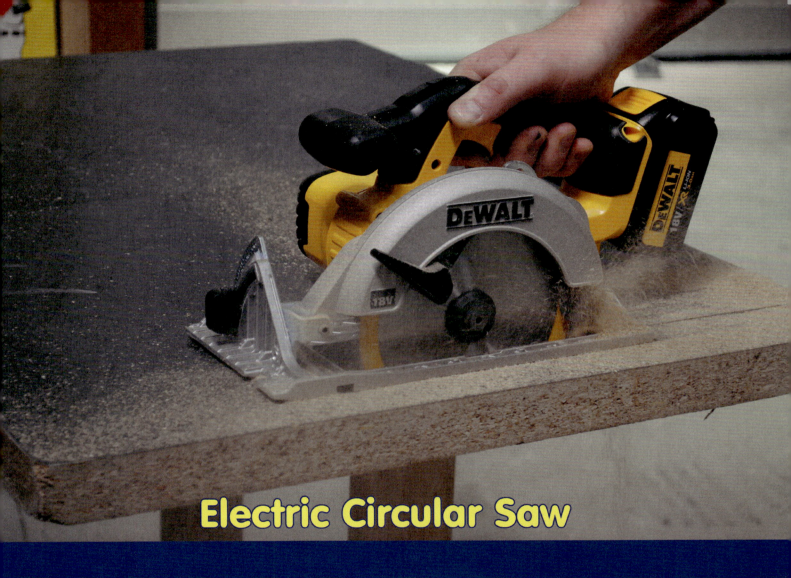

Electric Circular Saw

electric motors work. Just be sure they are unplugged from the outlet so you don't get shocked! Electricity is very powerful, so it's important to be careful even though we use it in our homes every day.

ELECTRICITY AND MAGNETISM WORK TOGETHER TO MAKE MOVEMENT

T he way a motor run by electricity works is rather simple. You plug it in to get the electrical current in, and then a metal rod, called an **axle**, spins to provide you with the power to run the machine.

Axle

Suppose you had a powerful horseshoe-shaped magnet. Then, you took a long piece of regular wire and formed a loop and placed it in between the magnet's poles. If you wrap each of the wire's two ends to a power source, such as a battery, something amazing will happen. The wire leaps up briefly. It looks magical, but there's actually a simple scientific reason.

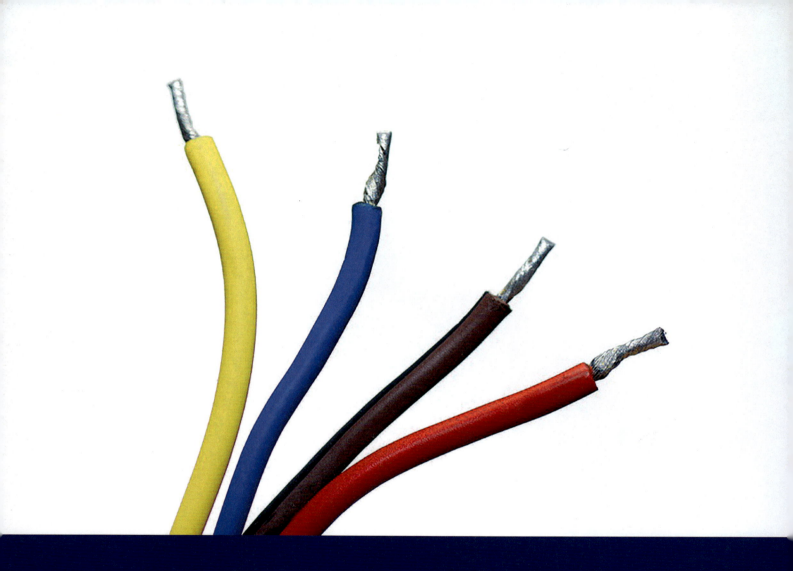

When you run a current of electricity on a wire, it makes an invisible field of magnetism around the wire. As you position the wire close to a magnet

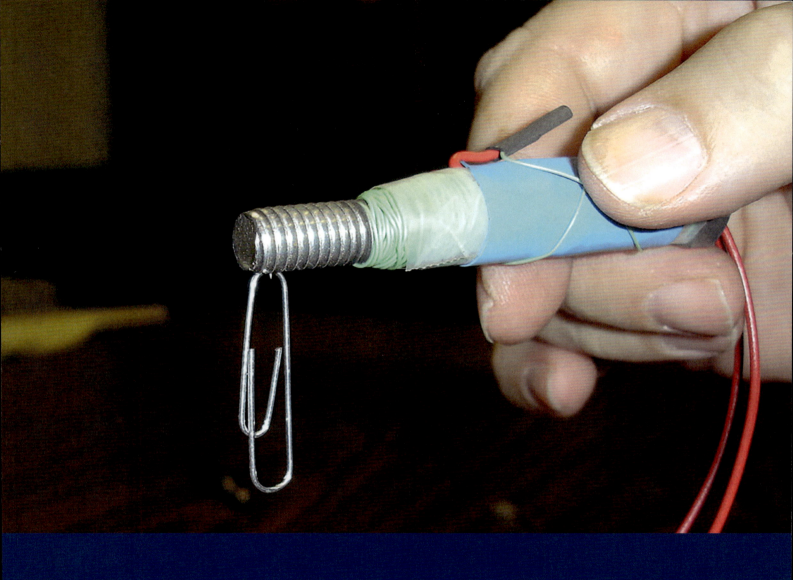

that's permanent, this temporary field of magnetism, the one you've created around the wire, reacts to the horseshoe magnet's field.

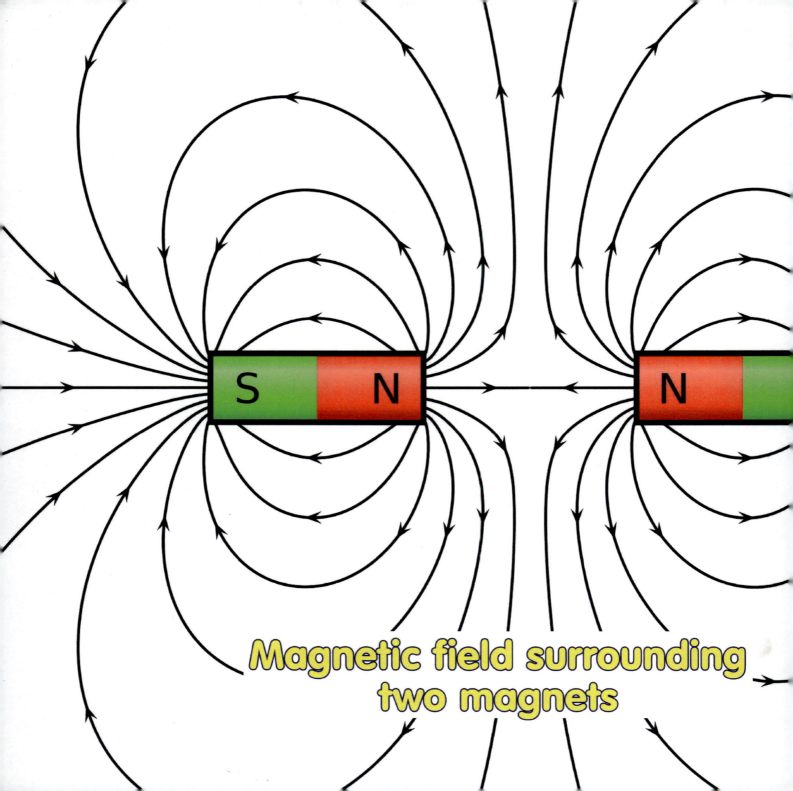

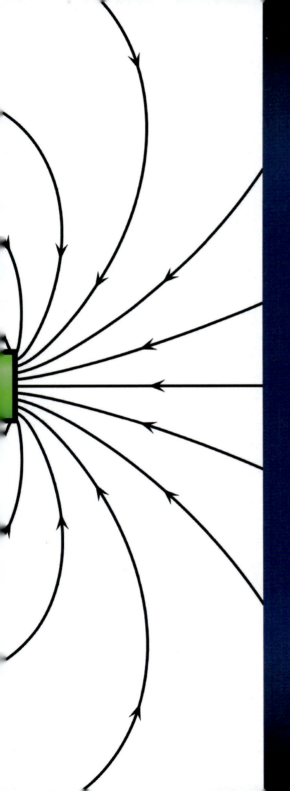

When you place two magnets next to each other, you can tell whether they attract each other or repel each other. The temporary magnetic field surrounding the wire works the same way. It either repels or attracts the magnetism coming from the horseshoe magnet, and that's what makes the jumping wire.

WHAT IS FLEMING'S LEFT-HAND RULE?

There's a rule to use to determine which way the wire, which is the electrical conductor, will jump using a memory aid and your left hand. It's called **Fleming's Left-Hand Rule**. Hold out your thumb and left hand's first finger, the one closest to your thumb, as if you were creating a gun.

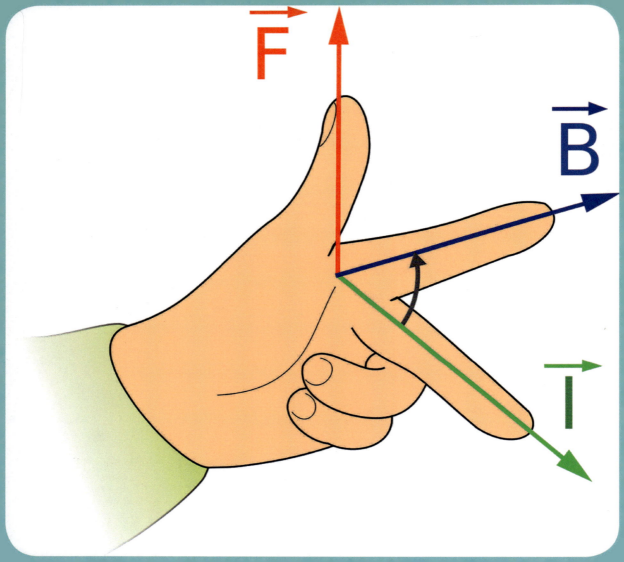

The two fingers should create a right angle. Now, bend the next finger, your second finger, at a right angle to your first. If you did this properly, all three of your fingers should be at 90-degree angles to each other. If you've studied geometry before, it's like an x, y, z coordinate system.

- The first finger will represent the magnetic field, F.
- The second finger will represent the electric current, C.
- Your thumb will represent the thrust, motion, or force of the conductor, M.

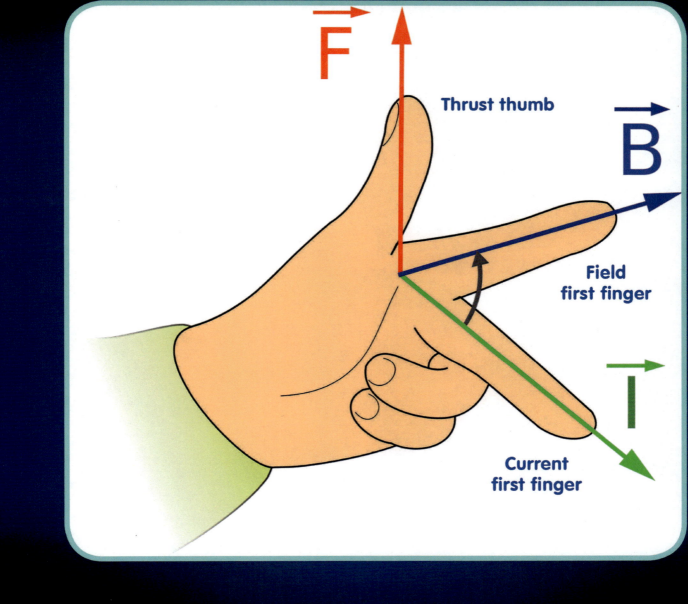

Now point your second finger the direction that the current is moving, which is from the battery's positive terminal to its negative terminal. At the same time, point your first finger toward the field's direction, which will be flowing from the magnet's North pole to its South pole. If you've pointed your second and first fingers correctly, your thumb will show you which direction the wire will move.

THE LINK BETWEEN ELECTRICITY, MAGNETISM AND MOVEMENT

In 1820, André-Marie Ampère, a French physicist, discovered the link that existed between electricity, movement, and fields of magnetism. This discovery became the foundation of the electric motor. However, it took the work of three inventors to come up with a practical way to use this discovery in a motor. Those inventors were Michael Faraday, William Sturgeon, and Joseph Henry.

André-Marie Ampère

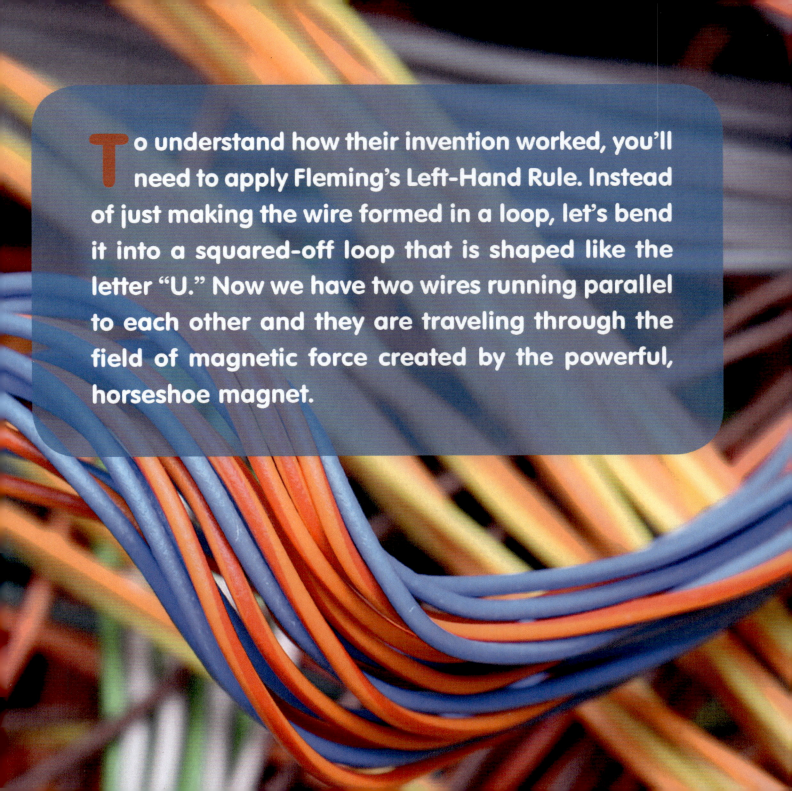

To understand how their invention worked, you'll need to apply Fleming's Left-Hand Rule. Instead of just making the wire formed in a loop, let's bend it into a squared-off loop that is shaped like the letter "U." Now we have two wires running parallel to each other and they are traveling through the field of magnetic force created by the powerful, horseshoe magnet.

One of the parts of the wire makes the current travel away from us, then it turns on the piece that is the bottom of the "U," and then the current comes back towards us. The Left-Hand Rule explains that these two parts of the wire will be moving opposite to each other. When the current is switched on and starts moving through the wire, one side of the "U" will move in the upwards direction and the other will move in the opposite direction, downwards.

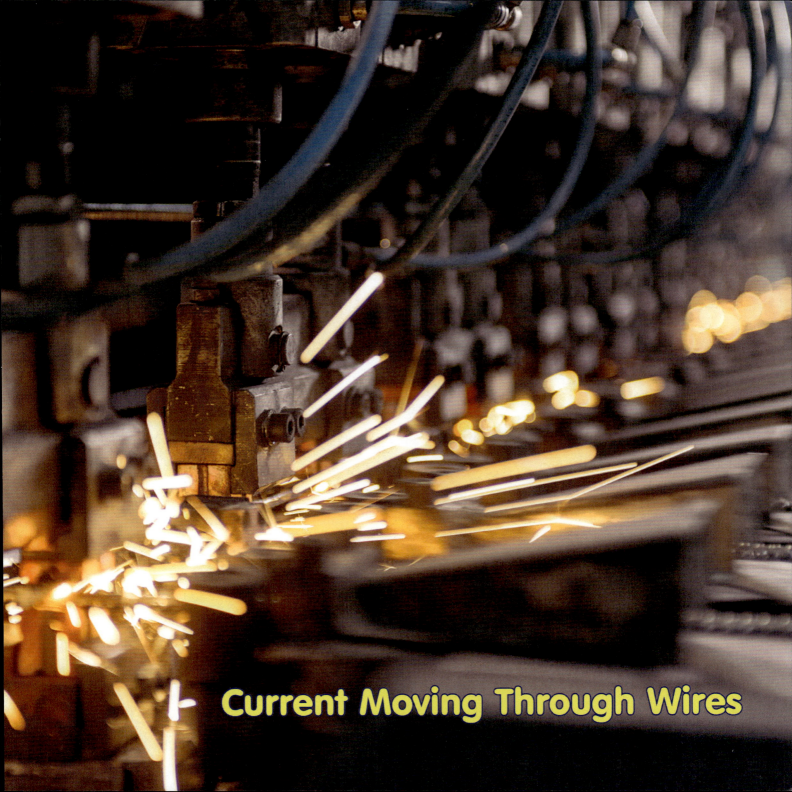

If the U-shaped wire coil would keep moving in this manner, it would be part of what we need to make an electric motor. However, the parallel wires would soon tangle together from the movement. Also, if it rotates too much, its movement would cause a problem as it gets into a vertical position.

Then, it would flip on itself, and the current would flow through in the opposite direction. The forces on each of the wire's sides would change direction. Instead of moving in the same direction continuously, it would move back and forth, out and then back again. An electric train with this kind of motion would just move back and forth and back and forth, without ever getting anywhere!

Electric Train

STABILIZING THE ELECTRIC MOTOR

There are two ways that inventors could see to solve this problem regarding the current changing direction. The two ways are:

- To use alternating current, which is a type of current that changes direction in a periodic cycle

- To use a special component, called a **commutator** to the wire coil's ends

For the small objects in our homes that use electric motors, a commutator is a simpler solution than using alternating current, also called AC. The technical term "commutator" is easy to remember since it comes from the word "commute." You may have heard of the commutative property in math class. Here the word "commute" just means to travel back and forth.

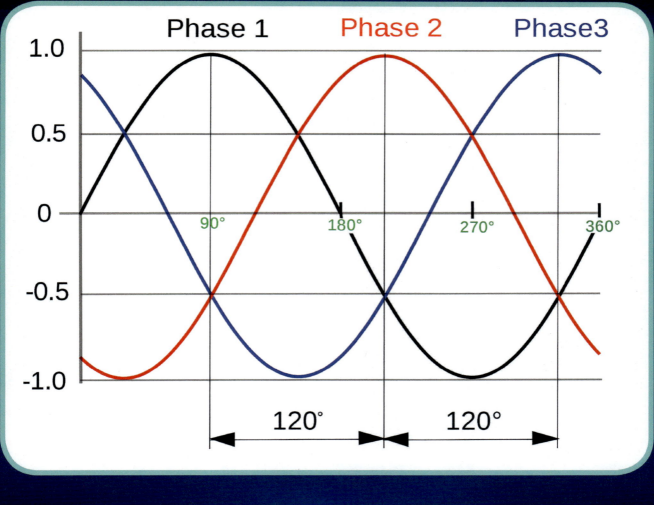

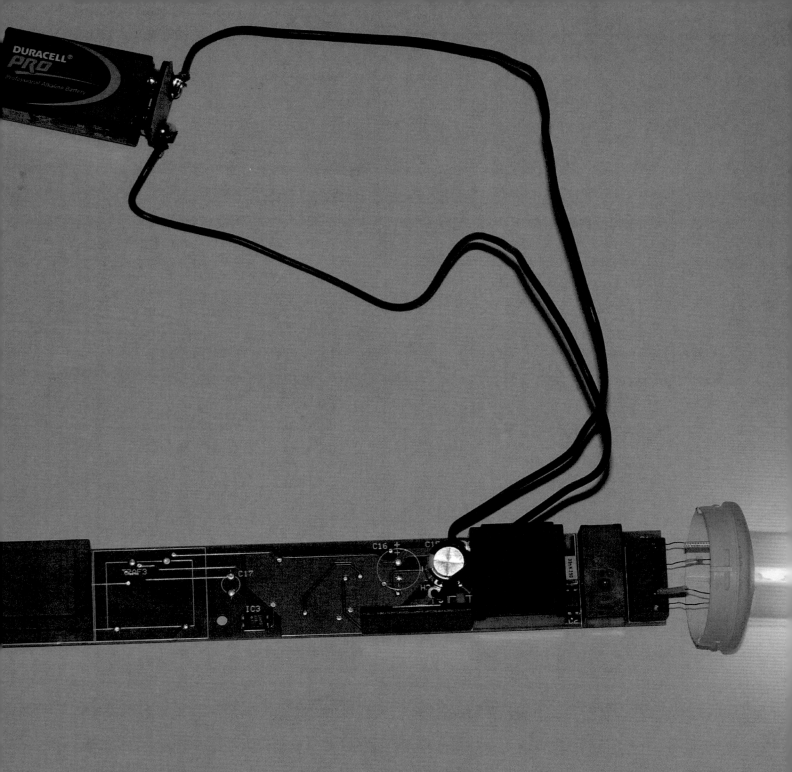

The simplest type of commutator is a ring made of metal that is separated into two halves. Its task is basic. It just makes the electrical current reverse direction every time there is a half turn of rotation. The two parallel parts of the wire are attached to each of the commutator's halves. The battery's electrical current connects to the terminals on the electric motor.

Power is fed into the commutator by two loose connections. These connectors are made from metal that is springy or graphite, like the "lead" in your pencil. They are called brushes because they brush against the commutator to send it electricity. Once the commutator is in position, when electricity flows through the U-shaped loop, called a circuit, the wire coil will always rotate in the same direction, instead of going back and forth.

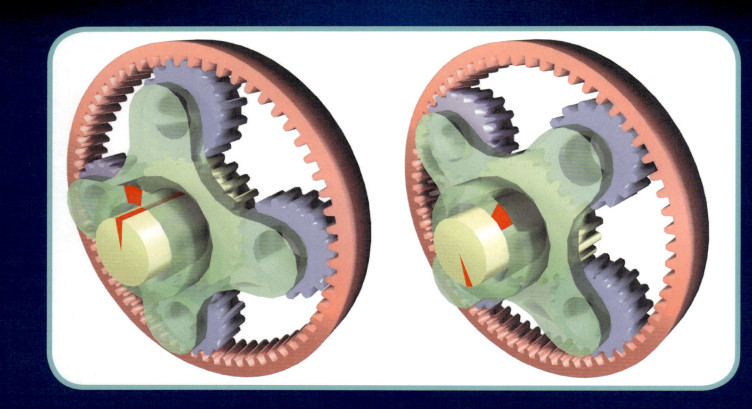

Gears Torque Multiplier

INCREASING THE POWER OF AN ELECTRIC MOTOR

Of course, simple electric motors can't generate that much power. If you want to increase the force of the turning, called torque, it can be done three different ways:

- Have more powerful, heavy-duty permanent magnets

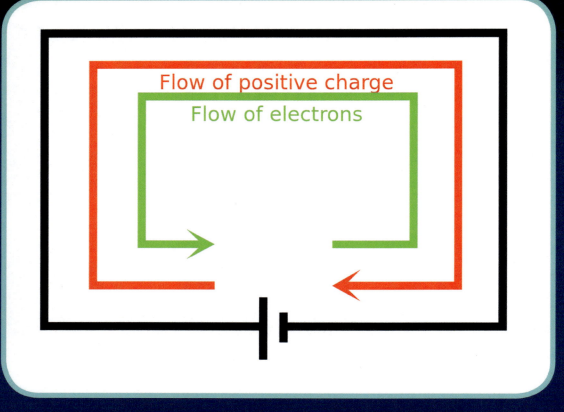

Current Notation

- Increase the flow of electrical current through the wire

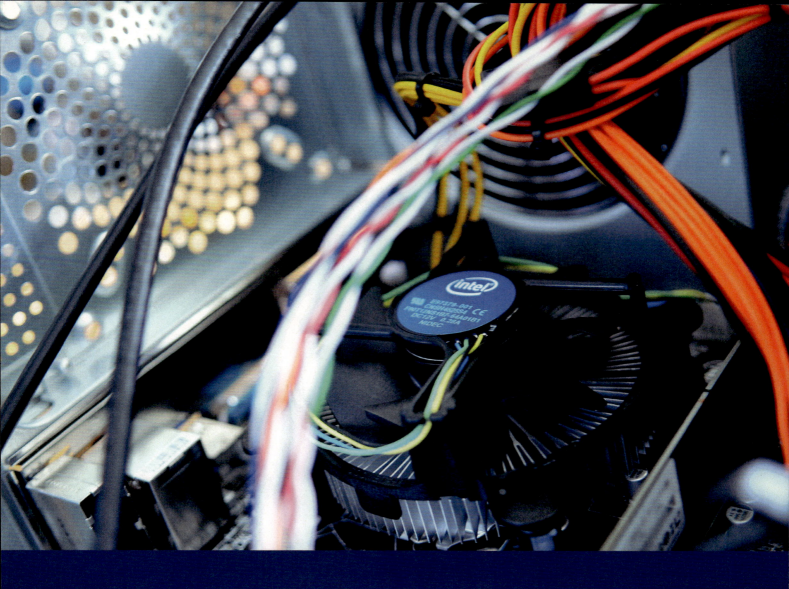

- Use many turns or loops of thin wire, instead of just one thicker wire

Also, motors are designed so that the permanent magnets are curved around the coils. That way they almost touch the wire coils that are rotating inside of them. The closer the magnets are to the coils, the more force the motor can create.

THE ESSENTIAL PARTS OF A DIRECT CURRENT MOTOR

Simple electric motors use direct current. They have two essential parts.

One or more permanent magnets are positioned inside the case. They don't move so they are static and called the motor's stator.

Stator Winding

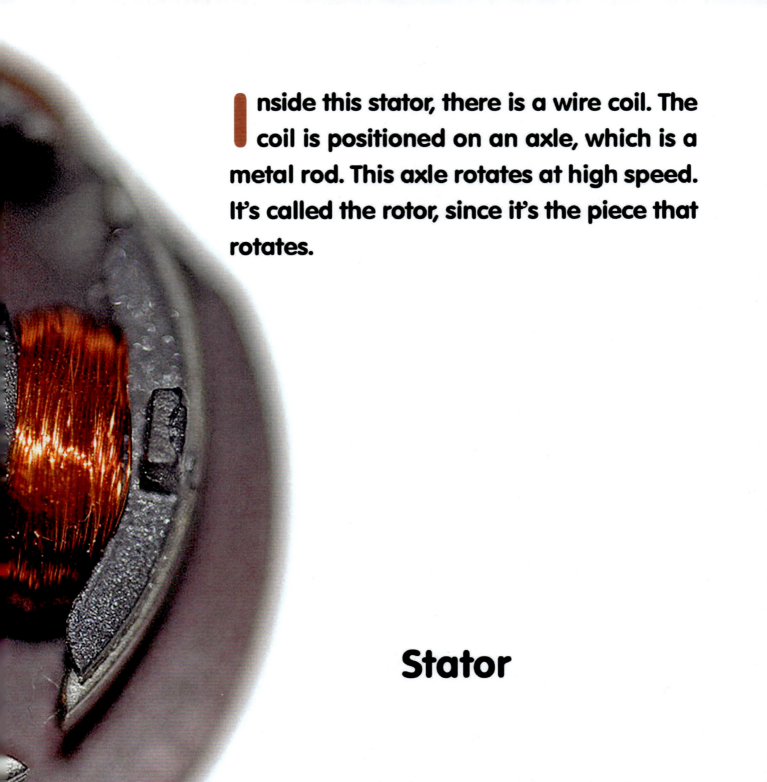

Inside this stator, there is a wire coil. The coil is positioned on an axle, which is a metal rod. This axle rotates at high speed. It's called the rotor, since it's the piece that rotates.

Stator

The rotor also has a commutator to keep the mechanism spinning in the same direction instead of just moving back and forth. The rotor is linked directly to the electrical power supply. These types of simple direct current motors are powerful enough for small toys and electric shavers.

Electric Mixer

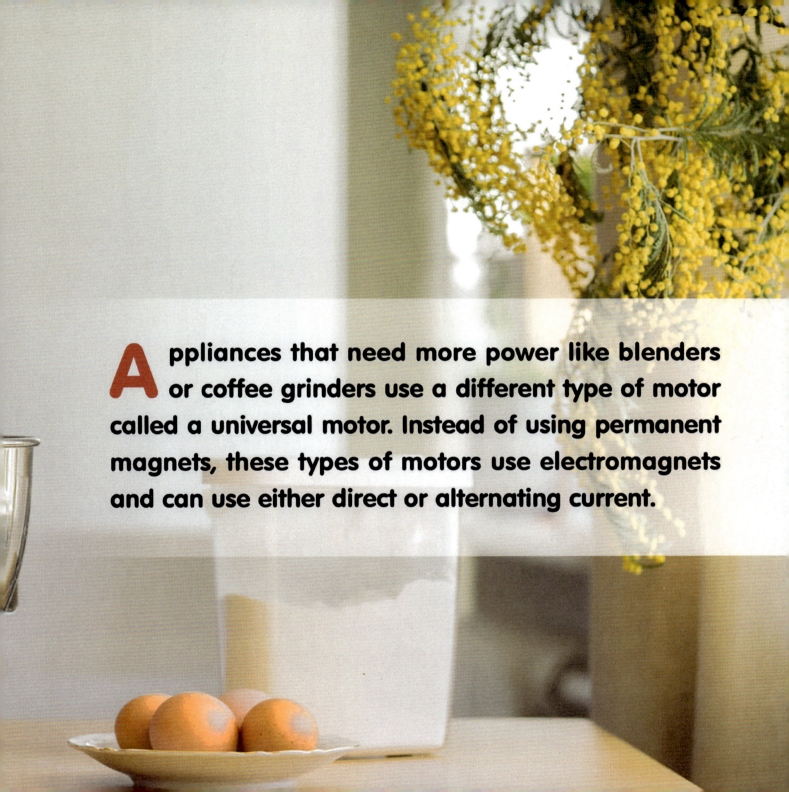

Appliances that need more power like blenders or coffee grinders use a different type of motor called a universal motor. Instead of using permanent magnets, these types of motors use electromagnets and can use either direct or alternating current.

SUMMARY

Electric motors are critical to almost everything we do in daily life. They work using some simple principles relating electricity and magnetism that took scientists many centuries to piece together. Electrical current flows through a wire coil, which subsequently creates a magnetic field. A permanent magnet influences the direction that the inner mechanism rotates and a commutator ensures that it rotates in the same direction.

Awesome! Now you know more about how electric motors work. You can find more Physics books from Baby Professor by searching the website of your favorite book retailer.